Cut to Shine!

Reflecting the Character of God

Annette E. Williams

STRENGTH IN CHRIST
— PUBLICATIONS —

Cut to Shine!

by Annette Williams

Copyright © 2017

Cover Design: Janet Dado

Unless otherwise noted scripture quotations are from *The Holy Bible. Authorized King James Version, Grand Rapids , MI, Zondervan, 2009.Print.*

International Standard Book Number: 978-0-9907963-1-2

Printed in the United States of America

Table of Contents

Dedicated to my wonderful husband Stephen who allows me the freedom to pursue my dreams and shine!

CUT TO SHINE!

Introduction

A life well lived is not for the faint hearted, it is full of difficult and challenging experiences from hard trials, to disappointment, to heartache, to injury and illness. The effect these have on an individual may result in a life of darkness and sorrow; a life that negatively affects all that come in contact with the person. Conversely, the difficult circumstances of life can produce an outcome that serves as a brilliant representation of the creator and a reflection of the character of God.

Developing the character of God takes time, experience and sacrifice. It can be likened to the process of cutting a diamond. Much like the examples Jesus used by likening the natural to understand the spiritual this book compares the diamond cutting process to the experience of the Christian believer.

A Christian believer is someone who has submitted their life to the lordship of Jesus Christ and lives as an example of Christ on earth.

We live as Born Again believers in the virgin birth, crucifixion and resurrection of Jesus Christ. Through the example of suffering that Christ endured for our salvation we are instructed in the word of God, the Bible, to allow the cutting circumstances of life to shape and fashion our lives in such a way that we reflect the light of Christ and shine brightly.

꧁꧂

Developing the character of God takes time, experience and sacrifice.

꧁꧂

To shine forth with God's glory it is important to get an understanding of what the glory of God is. Many believers are under the impression that the glory of God is an ethereal presence felt during high times of worship. Scripture teaches that the glory of God is actually His goodness; His character. Look at the passage from Exodus 33:12-19 where Moses asks God to reveal his glory.

[12]And Moses said unto the LORD, See, thou sayest unto me, Bring up this people: and thou hast not let me know whom thou wilt send with me. Yet thou hast said, I know thee by name, and

thou hast also found grace in my sight. [13]Now therefore, I pray thee, if I have found grace in thy sight, shew me now thy way, that I may know thee, that I may find grace in thy sight: and consider that this nation *is* thy people. [14]And he said, My presence shall go *with thee*, and I will give thee rest.[15]And he said unto him, If thy presence go not *with me*, carry us not up hence. [16]For wherein shall it be known here that I and thy people have found grace in thy sight? *is it* not in that thou goest with us? so shall we be separated, I and thy people, from all the people that *are* upon the face of the earth. [17]And the LORD said unto Moses, I will do this thing also that thou hast spoken: for thou hast found grace in my sight, and I know thee by name. [18]And he said, I beseech thee, shew me thy glory. [19]And he said, I will make all my goodness pass before thee, and I will proclaim the name of the LORD before thee; and will be gracious to whom I will be gracious, and will shew mercy on whom I will shew mercy.

Be encouraged to rise up and shine forth by reflecting the character of God in everything that you say and do. By learning the cutting process of a diamond may you allow God to create facets that shine with a brilliance.

Included are short biographies of individuals that shined or are currently shining like diamonds for the kingdom of God by allowing adversity to shape them. May these examples serve as an inspiration to you as you move forward in your own quest to shine forth.

*Arise, shine for thy light is come and the glory of the Lord is risen upon thee, **Isaiah 60:1***

This book is primarily written for the born again believer. Shining forth as God intended is not possible for a person who is lost in sin. It can be compared to a diamond in the dirt. The New Living Translation of Psalm 40:2 says He lifted me out of the pit of despair, out of the mud and the mire. When you are a sinner you are in the mud and mire and need to be lifted out before you can be cut to shine. If you have not repented and received the completed works of Jesus Christ making Him your personal Lord and Savior why not take the time to do so now? I encourage you to read the following prayer and accept Jesus into your life today.

Dear Jesus,

I acknowledge that I am a sinner and have fallen short of what You require of me. I have lived my life for myself and done things that please only me. I am sorry for this Lord and I

repent and I ask you to forgive me. I believe with my heart and I confess with my mouth that You were born of a virgin, crucified on the cross for me and resurrected from the dead. I come to you now and ask you to take control of my life; I give it fully to you. I believe I am now saved. Help me to live every day in a way that pleases you. It is in Your name I pray. Amen.

By saying this prayer from a sincere heart you have taken the first step to entering into the Kingdom of Heaven and becoming a born again Christian. Your next step is to seek out a Bible believing church that can nurture your new status as a citizen of heaven and help you grow and mature as a Christian.

Chapter 1

Why Cut to Shine?

One morning while spending time with God, I wrote in my journal that I have to learn to remain calm under **the pressure of uncomfortable situations**. God led me to read the entire book of James. After reading it completely three times by the leading of the Holy Spirit this is what I wrote in my journal:

James 3:17 Wisdom from above is first pure, then peaceable, gentle, and easy to be intreated, full of mercy and good fruits, without partiality, and without hypocrisy.

James 4:10 Humble yourselves in the sight of the Lord, and He shall lift you up.

James 1:2-4 [2]My brethren, count it all joy when ye fall into divers temptations; [3]Knowing this, that the trying of your faith worketh patience. [4] But let patience have her perfect work, that ye may be perfect and entire, wanting nothing.

Stand strong in temptations in **the pressure of uncomfortable situations** and allow patience to work; this is my opportunity to grow and mature. Embrace the pressure because it is pressure that produces a diamond.

I was intrigued by the statement *pressure produces a diamond*; why would I write this? Is it something I learned at some time in my life? I became so intrigued that I began to study diamonds to learn more about them; how they are formed, why they are highly valued and considered precious and rare. To my surprise, I found that the characteristics and formation of a diamond relate to the Christian walk and how God works in us to create the person He wants us to be.

Like a diamond we are *formed at high pressure*, we *have a cleavage plane*, we *can only be scratched by other diamonds, all diamonds have flaws* and are *cut and polished to reveal the highest brilliance*. Each of these characteristics and how they relate to our Christian walk will be explained in this book.

Diamonds are cut to bring out their brilliance and shine. Once cut the gemological industry uses the term "finish" which covers every aspect of a diamond's appearance that is not a result of the diamond's inherent nature when it comes out of the ground. In the same way, when you allow God to be the diamond cutter in your life you will shine forth like a finished diamond, reflecting the light and character of Jesus Christ.

By shining forth with the light and character of Jesus amazing things can happen that not only change you but also the world around you. God wants us to influence the world by shining forth with His glory. Again, I encourage you to allow yourself to be CUT TO SHINE!

Chapter 2

What is a Diamond

A diamond is hard, durable and has high optical dispersion (ability to disperse light of different colors) resulting in the luster of the stone. It is the hardest known natural material.

When we think about what it means to shine and think of various objects most of these shiny objects don't have their own source of light. They reflect light from another source. For example, the moon shines but only as a reflection of the Sun. A rock filled with certain minerals will also shine and reflect light. The most celebrated and valuable rock known to man is the diamond.

The diamond has been called "A girl's best friend" because it is the most popular gemstone and is used as a symbol of steadfast love. It is the hardest natural substance known to man and is used in various applications.

Many people think diamonds are formed from coal as it is what we are taught in science class, but diamonds are not formed from coal. Diamonds start out as diamonds as explained by Hobart King (Ph.D., M.S. Geology, West Virginia University; B.S. Geology, California University of Pennsylvania):

Methods of Diamond Formation (diamonds are not coal)

Many people believe that diamonds are formed from the metamorphism of coal. That idea continues to be the "how diamonds form" story in many science classrooms.

Coal has rarely played a role in the formation of diamonds. In fact, most diamonds that have been dated are much older than Earth's first land plants - the source material of coal! That alone should be enough evidence to shut down the idea that Earth's diamond deposits were formed from coal...

Geologists believe that the diamonds in all of Earth's commercial diamond deposits were formed in the mantle and delivered to the surface by deep-source volcanic eruptions. These eruptions produce the kimberlite and lamproite pipes that are sought after by diamond prospectors. Diamonds weathered and eroded from these eruptive deposits are now contained in the sedimentary (placer) deposits of streams and coastlines.

The formation of natural diamonds requires very high temperatures and pressures. These conditions occur in limited zones of Earth's mantle about 90 miles (150 kilometers) below the surface where temperatures are at least 2000 degrees Fahrenheit (1050 degrees Celsius). This critical temperature-pressure environment for diamond formation and stability is not present globally. Instead it is thought to be present primarily in the mantle beneath the stable interiors of continental plates.

Diamonds formed and stored in these "diamond stability zones" are delivered to Earth's surface during deep-source volcanic eruptions. These eruptions tear out pieces of the mantle and carry them rapidly to the surface, This type of volcanic eruption is extremely rare and has not occurred since scientists have been able to recognize them.

Is coal involved? Coal is a sedimentary rock, formed from plant debris deposited at Earth's surface. It is rarely buried to depths greater than two miles (3.2 kilometers). It is very unlikely that coal has been moved from the crust down to a depth well below the base of a continental plate. The carbon source for these mantle diamonds is most likely carbon trapped in Earth's interior at the time of the planet's formation...

The Most Convincing Evidence

The most convincing evidence that coal did not play a role in the formation of most diamonds is a comparison between the age of Earth's diamonds and the age of the earliest land plants...

Since coal is formed from terrestrial plant debris and the oldest land plants are younger than almost every diamond that has ever been dated, it is easy to conclude that coal did not play a significant role in the formation of Earth's diamonds. [1]

Diamonds start out as a natural crystal. They have reflective properties that are brought out by craftsmen that know how to cut the diamond to create the most brilliance. It is a mistake to believe that Diamonds are made from coal; they actually start as diamonds, not coal. This is important to understand because it qualifies my

---

[1] *Excerpt: http://geology.com/articles/diamonds-from-coal/12 January 2015 Wikipedia contributors. "Diamond." Wikipedia, The Free Encyclopedia. Wikipedia, The Free Encyclopedia, 27 Dec. 2014. Web. 12 Jan. 2015.*

comparison of the Christian believer to the diamond in that we all start out as diamonds with the ability to shine.

It's easy to see how people think diamonds are made from coal, since they are made from compressed carbon atoms, and coal is almost completely composed of carbon (along with hydrogen, sulfur, oxygen, nitrogen, and some other stuff).

Only one problem: Diamonds are formed way deeper into the earth than coal. Coal is formed in the crust (because remember, it comes from plants, even the oldest of which are still relatively close to earth's surface), whereas diamonds are formed in the upper mantle, which sits just below the crust. Diamonds are carried to the surface through a molten mantle-rock called Kimberlite, which travels through the crust and explodes from the surface in (relatively) small volcano-like eruptions. Coal, however, just kind of sits there until we dig it up.

So there you have it. Coal is mostly carbon, diamonds are made of carbon, but this is one case where $A + B \neq C$.[2]

---

[2] *"Diamonds Aren't Made From Coal." The NeverNoob. N.p., 11 Apr. 2014. Web. 06 May 2017.*

We can be comforted in knowing that God made us unique and precious from the start. We were never some black ugly lump of coal but a brilliant diamond ready to be revealed.

> *[14]I will praise thee; for I am fearfully and wonderfully made: marvellous are thy works; and that my soul knoweth right well. Psalm 139:14*

With this truth about the origin of diamonds let's take a look at how diamonds are formed.

Chapter 3

How Are Diamonds Formed?

Formed at high pressure; 87-120 miles below the ground. It is thrust from its depth by volcanic activity.

You could say that diamonds are propelled from the earth under extreme pressure. In comparison, we are propelled to shine forth by extreme pressure. As a Christian believer, we identify with Christ. The suffering that He endured on His way to the cross produced a reflection of God's character like no other.

When we embrace the pressure that God puts us through and face it with the instruction of God's word we too become beautiful reflections of His character.

Scripture instructs us to endure the temptations and pressure:

Blessed is the man that endureth temptation: for when he is tried, he shall receive the crown of life, which the Lord hath promised to them that love him. *James 1:12*

^{6} Wherein ye greatly rejoice, though now for a season, if need be, ye are in heaviness through manifold temptations:

^{7} That the trial of your faith, being much more precious than of gold that perisheth, though it be tried with fire, might be found unto praise and honour and glory at the appearing of Jesus Christ: *1 Peter 1:6-7*

A deeper study of the word glory in this verse reveals it is translated from the Greek word doxa with splendor and brightness as part of its definition. We are to be found shining forth with brightness when Jesus returns having been tried with fire.

My brethren, count it all joy when ye fall into divers temptations; *James 1:2*

Knowing this, that the trying of your faith worketh patience. *James 1:3*

But let patience have her perfect work, that ye may be perfect and entire, wanting nothing. *James 1:4*

The scientific community does not have an exact measure of how long it takes a diamond to form. Estimates are in the 1 billion to 3.3 billion year range[3]. Needless to say, it takes a very long time. We can be assured that it won't take us that long to become the reflection of God's character however it does take time and we must allow God to work on us however long it takes.

The perfect work of patience is permanence of character; love, joy, peace, forbearance (patience), kindness, goodness, faithfulness, gentleness, and self-control which are the fruits of the spirit. When we have these characteristics we are reflecting to the world the glory of God.

Letting patience have her perfect work is an act of surrender. The same surrender that Jesus yielded to in the Garden of Gethsemane; "not my will but thy will be done" *Luke 22:42*.

It's difficult to let go of our will and allow God to cut us as He sees fit, however, we must remember during times of pressure that God by the Holy Spirit is bringing out the beautiful diamond He created us to become.

---

[3]Wikipedia contributors. "Diamond." *Wikipedia, The Free Encyclopedia.* Wikipedia, The Free Encyclopedia, 20 May. 2017. Web. 26 May. 2017.

Chapter 4

The Rough Stage

The Cleavage Plane

Diamonds have a cleavage plane, a place created during its formation that is more fragile than others. Diamond cutters often use this attribute to cleave (cut; break) the stone prior to faceting. If it is cut wrong it will be crushed into tiny pieces.

What is your cleavage plane or breaking point? It is where your will comes up against God's will. You must yield and allow Him to break you so that He can create facets that make you shine.

Our soul; mind, will, and emotions, is being changed by the process of allowing God to break us each time an issue comes up that does not line up with God's will; the fragile place of decision to do what you know to be right.

You must yield and allow Him to break you
so that He can create facets to make you
shine.

What areas in your life are more fragile than others? What action do you take that you know it is against the word of God but to deny yourself the pleasure of it would cause you to suffer or be in pain? It is that area that is your cleavage plane. God wants to break us in this area and if we allow Him to we will be much stronger and able to resist the temptation to go against the word of God.

Don't concern yourself that God will put more pressure than you can bear. An important reality about a diamond is that it heats quickly and cannot remain on the cutting wheel for long stretches of time. We are comforted by 1 Corinthians 10:13; There hath no temptation taken hold of you but such as is common to man. But God is faithful; He will not suffer you to be tempted beyond that which ye are able to bear, but with the temptation will also make a way to escape, that ye may be able to bear it.

Our ability to bear up under the cutting process is an act of our will; when we allow God to have control. The spiritual fruits of longsuffering and self-control are developed through the cutting process.

> The sacrifices of God are a broken spirit: a broken and a contrite heart, O God, thou wilt not despise. *Psalm 51:17*

God in His mercy will allow us to experience the same struggles over and over again until we come to the place of full and true submission; the place where we allow God to break us and shape us. If we refuse to be broken then we face the possibility of being crushed by the very thing that could have made us shine.

Many times this place of brokenness is fueled by people around us; friends, family and sometimes even strangers; which brings us to another way the diamond is cut, by other diamonds.

Only Scratched by Other Diamonds

> *It is so hard it can only be scratched by another diamond. It is so tough it has the ability to resist breakage from forceful impact. When a diamond*

*scratches another diamond damage can occur in
one or both stones.*

Being shaped within the hand of God polishes and creates
beautiful facets versus being damaged. God uses other
diamonds; our brothers and sisters in Christ to shape and
perfect us.

*The diamond can be split by a single, well
calculated blow of a hammer to a pointed tool,
which is quick, but risky. Alternatively, it can be
cut with a diamond saw, which is a more reliable
but tedious procedure. Because when a diamond
scratches another diamond damage can occur in
one or both of the stones.*

The diamond saw represents other believers shaping the
diamond (us) **by the hand of God** (the diamond cutter)
creating a beautiful facet instead of damage.

Scripture tells us in Proverbs 27:17 that as iron
sharpeneth iron; so a man sharpeneth the countenance of
his friend. Likewise, diamonds cut other diamonds. Often
this experience is uncomfortable and difficult to bear but
how we respond is the key to becoming the diamond God
desires.

Another person may rub us the wrong way and by doing so we can either let them ruffle our feathers or allow that rub to be the file that smoothes out a sharp edge that is a part of our character. The very thing that causes another person to bring us to a boiling point may be the very thing that brings out the best in our character.

∽∾

The very thing that causes another person to bring us to a boiling point may be the very thing that brings out the best in our character.

∽∾

Please be cautioned that a diamond is the only precious stone said to be able to leave an indelible mark – never to be removed or forgotten. Therefore it is important that we as believers shape each other within the hand of God versus scratching each other on our own. Allow the leading of the Holy Spirit to guide you in relating to one another.

Always keep in mind the fruit of the spirit – the character of God that we are to reflect as we interact with others: love, joy, peace, forbearance (patience), kindness, goodness, faithfulness, gentleness, and self-control.

Further study of these characteristics will help you recognize when you fall short. Confess your error to God and ask Him to help you overcome. Be humble (teachable) and willing to endure the cutting process and experience God's handiwork in your life.

Humble confidence is what God desires of us and it comes from forming our identity and calling away from ourselves and placing them in Christ Jesus. In other words, just sit back, allow God to cut us even when it's through others and reflect the light of Jesus with the display of Godly character.

All Diamonds have Flaws

Most diamonds contain visible flaws that the diamond cutter has to decide which to keep and which are to be removed by cutting.

The extreme hardness and high value of a diamond means that the gem is typically polished slowly using painstaking traditional techniques and greater attention to detail than most other gemstones.

Diamonds are carefully analyzed before any cuts are made because they are brittle and can be split up with a single blow. Most contain visible flaws that the diamond cutter has to decide which to keep and which are to be removed by cutting.

Ask God what flaws are to remain in you. What flaws does He desire to cut away? Some flaws are to remain for His glory. Look at what Paul said in 2 Corinthians 12:7 10

> *[7] And lest I should be exalted above measure through the abundance of the revelations, there was given to me a thorn in the flesh, the messenger of Satan to buffet me, **lest I should be exalted above measure.** [8] For this thing I besought the Lord thrice, that it might depart from me. [9] And he said unto me, My grace is sufficient for thee: for my strength is made perfect in weakness. Most gladly therefore will I rather glory in my infirmities, that the power of Christ may rest upon me. [10] Therefore I take pleasure in infirmities, in reproaches, in necessities, in persecutions, in distresses for Christ's sake: for when I am weak, then am I strong.*

Flaws that are not removed are often hidden by the way they are set; in gold, platinum or silver in order to protect them.

It's important to note that gold symbolizes deity, God. A diamond set in gold can be compared to the believer set in the hand of God. We can be confident in knowing the God hides our flaws within the strength of His grace and protects us. Grace is defined as a giving of something that is undeserved. We don't deserve to have our flaws hidden but God's strength is made perfect in our weakness and He graces us with the ability to shine brilliantly despite our flaws.

We must remember that it is God's grace that gives us this ability and not ourselves lest we should be exalted above measure. In other words, in case we want to be prideful. Pride can make our witness dull much like a rough spot on a diamond which is why the process continues to make certain the diamond fully reflects the light.

Chapter 7
Preparing for Brilliance

Polishing the Stone

After cutting and splitting, the next step is polishing the stone. This removes rough material by gradual erosion and is extremely time consuming. Not all diamonds have the rough material removed, but it is only when it is removed and the diamond is cut will it be able to fully reflect the light.

Back to James 1:4 **"Let patience have her perfect work"**.

No one wants to suffer. It's difficult and it hurts. Everything in us rejects it because of the pain. We feel so bad that we forget what it feels like to be without the pain and the uncomfortable feeling overwhelms us. We can try to dull the pain; sleep through the pain – we find every way we can to get rid of the pain – but sometimes; most of the time; we have to suffer through the pain to get to the beauty on the other side. We are shaped by adversity and many times the beauty that is revealed is not for us but for someone else. Facets are developed during our suffering and pain that reflect the light of our heavenly Father as we allow it to. A light that shines for the world to see and the world is attracted to shiny things.

Think about how many people want diamonds, "Oh it shines so pretty, let me have the biggest one." They are drawn to the brilliance of how it reflects the light. The light shines upon those that are stuck in darkness drawing them closer to admire the light and desire it for themselves.

❧

Very few people have great light without great suffering of some kind.

❧

It's difficult to think of suffering for the sake of others. We know and appreciate the suffering Jesus went through and the sacrifice He made. But have you stopped to think about the suffering of the woman with an issue of blood? Her suffering and her story have been the inspiration for many faith walks, many healings, and even the inspiration for songs that have helped countless lives throughout history and continues even to this day. Her miraculous healing at the hem of Jesus' garment would not have had the same impact if she had not suffered all those years; something to really think about.

Study the miracles that are recorded in the Bible and you will discover that some form of suffering took place before the miracle was manifested. We often want a quick fix, immediate comfort and we don't want to suffer – even Jesus didn't want to suffer as evidenced by his agony in the Garden of Gethsemane – but oh the beauty that comes when we do; beauty that shines beyond our own capabilities.

Very few people have great light without great suffering of some kind. When you research the lives of people who have made a great impact for the kingdom of God you find they have been through great suffering. Diamonds don't shine with full luster until they are cut and faceted by a jeweler. God has been the master jeweler for the following people who suffered greatly in various forms and afterward reflected the great light of the kingdom with brilliance.

You are a diamond, reflecting the light of Jesus and it's time for you to shine. Realize the precious jewel you are and take inspiration from the diamonds that follow.

Chapter 9

Hidden Diamonds

Corrie ten Boom

The life of Corrie ten Boom is one that shines forth with the character of God. She was cut by dire circumstances few can fathom and yet her example brought many into the kingdom of God because the facets of her life reflected the love of Jesus in the dark days of the holocaust.

During World War II, the ten Booms lived out their Christian faith by making their home a refuge--a hiding place--for Jews and members of the Dutch underground who were being hunted by the Nazis.

Through these activities, the ten Boom family and their many friends saved the lives of an estimated 800 Jews, and protected many Dutch underground workers.

On February 28, 1944, the Gestapo (the Nazi secret police) raided their home. Because Nazi soldiers found underground materials and extra ration cards in their home, the ten Boom family was imprisoned. Corrie and her sister Betsie spent 10 months in three different prisons, the last being the infamous Ravensbruck concentration camp located near Berlin, Germany. Life in the camp was almost unbearable, but Corrie and Betsie spent their time sharing Jesus' love with their fellow prisoners. Many women became Christians in that terrible place because of Corrie and Betsie's witness to them. Betsie (59) died in Ravensbruck, but Corrie survived. She realized her life was a gift from God, and she needed to share what she and Betsie had learned in Ravensbruck: "There is no pit so deep that God's love is not deeper still," and "God will give us the love to be able to forgive our enemies." At age 53, Corrie began a worldwide ministry that took her into more than 60 countries in the next 32 years! She testified to God's love and encouraged all she met with the message that "Jesus is Victor."

In the early 1970's, Corrie's book *The Hiding Place* became a best seller, and World Wide Pictures (Billy Graham Evangelistic Association) released the major motion picture "The Hiding Place." Corrie was a woman faithful to God. She died on her 91st birthday, April 15, 1983. [4]

---

[4] *Excerpted from About the Ten Booms*. N.p., n.d. Web. 05 Apr. 2017.

Harriet Tubman

Harriet Tubman is another hidden diamond that shined forth during an equally horrendous time in history, the time of American slavery. Although she suffered from disabling epileptic seizures and headaches that were caused from being beaten and hit in the head with a heavy metal weight at the age of 15 she shined forth with a brilliance that led to the salvation of many lives.

Harriet Tubman was known by many as "Black Moses" because she delivered many of her people from the grips of slavery just as Moses delivered the children of Israel from the rule of Pharaoh. She has been quoted as saying she would listen carefully to the voice of God as she led slaves north, and she would only go where she felt God was leading her. Fellow abolitionist Thomas Garrett said of her, "I never met any person of any color who had more confidence in the voice of God."

Harriet Tubman escaped from slavery in the South to become a leading abolitionist before the American Civil War. She was born into slavery in Maryland in 1820, and successfully escaped in 1849. Yet she risked her life and freedom and returned many times to rescue both family members and other slaves from the plantation *system. Tubman led hundreds to freedom in the North as the most famous "conductor" on the Underground Railroad, an elaborate secret network of safe houses organized for that purpose. She also helped the Union Army during the war, working as a spy among other roles. After the Civil War ended, Tubman dedicated her life to helping impoverished former slaves and the elderly, establishing her own Home for the Aged. In honor of her life and by popular demand via an online poll, in 2016, the U.S. Treasury Department announced that Harriet Tubman will replace Andrew Jackson on the center of a new $20 bill.*

"I always tole God, 'I'm gwine [going] to hole stiddy on you, an' you've got to see me through.'"[5]

---

[5] *"Harriet Tubman." Biography.com. A&E Networks Television, 05 Jan. 2017. Web. 05 Apr. 2017.*

Halvorsen, Karen, Matt Donnelly, and A. G. Miller. "Harriet Tubman." Christian History | Learn the History of Christianity & the Church. N.p., n.d. Web. 07 Apr. 2017.

Chapter 10

A Diamond Cut by Error?

Fanny Jane Crosby

How many times have you heard or even sung yourself the following hymns; *Draw Me Nearer, Jesus Keep Me Near the Cross* and one of my favorites, *Blessed Assurance* also titled *This is My Story*?

> *This is my story, this is my song; praising my savior all the day long. This is my story this is my song; praising my savior all the day long.*

The writer of these and many others is a diamond that was cut as a child at the hands of an incompetent doctor.

As a baby, Frances Jane Crosby born March 24, 1820, had an eye infection which an incompetent doctor treated by placing hot poultices on her red and inflamed eyelids. The infection did clear up, but the result was that scars formed on her eyes, and Fanny became blind for life.

But although Fanny was blind, she did not consider herself handicapped. She did many of the things other children did and accepted her blindness with a positive attitude.

About her blindness, Fanny said:

"It seemed intended by the blessed providence of God that I should be blind all my life, and I thank him for the dispensation. If perfect earthly sight were offered me tomorrow I would not accept it. I might not have sung hymns to the praise of God if I had been distracted by the beautiful and interesting things about me."

If I had a choice, I would still choose to remain blind...for when I die, the first face I will ever see will be the face of my blessed Saviour."

Fanny Crosby was probably the most prolific hymnist in history, writing over 8,000 hymns. As many as 200 different pen names were given to her works by hymn book publishers so that the public wouldn't know she wrote so large a number of them. She produced as many as seven hymns/poems in one day. On several occasions, upon hearing an unfamiliar hymn sung, she would inquire about the author, and find it to be one of her own!

Fanny passed away on Feb. 12, 1915, and yet in many churches she continues to shine forth in the music she wrote. Fanny Crosby was one of the best-known women in the United States and a strong Christian whose legacy of faithfulness to God is exhibited by the hymns that will be sung for all eternity![6]

---

[6] "Faith Hall of Fame - Fanny Crosby." *Faith Hall of Fame - Fanny Crosby*. N.p., n.d. Web. 05 Apr. 2017.

"Fanny Crosby: America's Hymn Queen." *Christianity.com*. N.p., n.d. Web. 07 Apr. 2017.

Chapter 12
A Pearl that Shines like a Diamond

Pearl Fryar

While watching television one Saturday afternoon I came across a documentary entitled *A Man Named Pearl*. This movie depicted the life of a sharecropper's son who created an internationally renowned topiary garden without ever attending a formal class on the art of topiary. The story was fascinating and prompted me to want to visit Pearl's amazing topiary garden. I was encouraged by the fact that the garden was close enough for a day trip. I didn't know at the time that it would take 10 years before we made the trip.

Then seemingly out of the blue I was reminded of this wonder tucked away in a small South Carolina town and I planned the trip. When we arrived we were the only patrons that morning in spite of the fact that the garden attracts over 5,000 annual visitors.

My anticipation and excitement to experience the garden were not let down. We slowly walked around taking in all of the intricate creations. Pearl's garden promotes the message of love, peace, and goodwill and these words are displayed in artistic creations throughout his garden.

As we marveled at the creations and wondered about the countless hours that each must have taken to achieve we were given a wonderful surprise. An older gentleman rode up alongside us in a yard tractor; it was Pearl Fryar himself! We were blessed to engage him in conversation and he patiently told us the story of his creation.

The genesis of this remarkable garden started with his initial desire to win yard of the month. He visited a local nursery and saw a sculpted plant that piqued his interest. He was briefly shown by a worker how he could cut a juniper like that himself and he took home a plant that was headed to the garbage pile to practice on. Pearl planted, cared for and shaped the plant using his own sense of style. From that small plant, he began planting and shaping junipers throughout his yard and the rest is history.

Pearl painstakingly cuts each plant and his efforts have created a masterpiece of artwork that students worldwide seek to learn from. While there he told us about a group of students that would be arriving from England to study his unique procedure of creating his abstract art.

Pearl Fryar's garden has allowed him to shine like a diamond with far reaching brilliance. He gave us a copy of the local newspaper that contained a recent article about his passionate philanthropic project. The article detailed the 2016 recipients of The Pearl Fryar Scholarship. He explained that there are many high school students that work hard in school and have average passing grades. Unfortunately, the scholarships are often reserved for those with the highest GPAs.

The Pearl Fryar Scholarship Fund gives average students with creative abilities encouragement to pursue and achieve their dreams of success. His quote from his website explains it best:

"I was an average student academically; that's where I came from...Then I created this garden that's internationally known. It shows that a kid who is average academically can still make important contributions to our society. I want people to be aware of that. I want to be able to encourage those students that don't always get the attention that may give them the courage to go after their own dreams." [7]

---

[7] Pearl Fryar, http://www.pearlfryar.com

We lingered in the hot sun and spoke with Mr. Fryar for almost an hour as sweat poured down our faces. The reflection of character from this diamond glistened in our presence. His passion, dedication, and strong focus inspired me even the more to allow the cuts of the hard times that I've had to endure reflect the brilliance of Christ's character in my own life.

I encourage you to learn more about Mr. Pearl Fryar and visit his garden; you too may be encouraged to shine brighter.

Chapter 12

The Most Brilliant Diamond

The honor of "Most Rare and Expensive Gem" goes to the Pink Star Diamond. This stunning beauty weighs in at a hefty 59.6 carats. When it was put up on Sotheby's auction block in 2013, the Pink Star went for a jaw-dropping $83.2 million. However the auction winner defaulted on the payment and this vivid pink diamond now sits in Sotheby's inventory, valued at $72 million. This valuation puts the Pink Star in at $1,208,053.69 per carat.[8]

This diamond is here on earth and its value is based on its rarity and beauty. The monetary value of this gem can vary as noted based on what an individual chooses to pay.

This earthly diamond pales in comparison to the most brilliant diamond in the Kingdom of God, Jesus Christ!

---

[8] *"Top 10 Rarest Gemstones." The Loupe | TrueFacet. N.p., 06 Feb. 2017. Web. 16 Feb. 2017.*

As God's only Son Jesus was fashioned and formed for our benefit. Isaiah 53:10 says that it pleased God to bruise Jesus;

Yet it pleased the LORD to bruise him; he hath put him to grief: when thou shalt make his soul an offering for sin, he shall see his seed, he shall prolong his days, and the pleasure of the LORD shall prosper in his hand. **Isaiah 53:10**

If is pleased the Lord God to bruise Jesus, His beloved Son to bring us back to full relationship with Him; how much more does it please Him to bruise us to become like Jesus? We are to take up our cross daily and suffer with Jesus; something many pastors, teacher and leaders don't tell us.

ço~ல

For once you were full of darkness, but now you have light from the Lord. So live as people of light! Ephesians 5:8 NLT

ço~ல

However to develop the character that Jesus portrays we must allow God to shape us and cut us and bring us to a place of brilliance.

Jesus shines with love the greatest character we can have as it is love that governs all the other characteristics of God. If we function in the love that Jesus gives as an example, the kind of love that is unconditional, we will function in all of the other fruits of the spirit as well.

The fruits of love, joy, peace, forbearance (patience), kindness, goodness, faithfulness, gentleness and self-control shine forth when we allow God to shape us. These fruit are the glory of God. As He tells us in Isaiah 60:1-2, Arise, shine; for thy light is come, and the glory of the Lord is risen upon thee. [2]For, behold, the darkness shall cover the earth, and gross darkness the people: but the Lord shall arise upon thee, and **his glory shall be seen upon thee**.

Daily Use

Diamonds are popular in engagement and wedding rings because they can withstand daily use.

God desires to use you daily to shine forth. Matthew 5:16 Let your light so shine before men, that they may see your good works and glorify the Father which is in heaven. To have this light, which is a reflection of His light, with the brilliance God desires you must endure the pressure of being cut, split, polished and set. The setting supports and protects the stone and allows it to be safely carried from place to place. The setting in a Christian's life can be compared to being carried by God the Father and having a foundation in the word of God.[9]

> Isaiah 60: 1-2, Arise, shine; for thy light is come, and the glory of the Lord is risen upon thee. [2]For, behold, the darkness shall cover the earth, and gross darkness the people: but the Lord shall arise upon thee, and **his glory shall be seen upon thee.**

In conclusion I'll share with you a very encouraging poem from a lovely 92 year old woman, Wanda B. Goines. She can be found on YouTube.com beautifully and emotionally reciting her poem. Please allow her poem to be an inspiration for you to allow the cutting of God to create facets to shine forth with Godly character not only in eternity but throughout the rest of your days here on earth.

---

[9] You can learn more on developing a foundation (the diamond's setting) by reading my first book, *A Sure Foundation, Stability Through Life's Storms*. Available online at https://www.createspace.com/4943915. Enter discount code WCKHKPEA for $5.00 off.

The Gift Wrap and the Jewel

"I looked in the mirror and what did I see,

but a little old lady peering back at me.

With bags and sags and wrinkles and wispy white hair,

and I asked my reflection, how did you get there?

You once were straight and vigorous and now you're stooped and weak.

When I tried so hard to keep you from becoming an antique.

My reflection's eyes twinkled as she solemnly replied,

you're looking at the gift wrap and not the jewel inside.

A living gem and precious of unimagined worth.

Unique and true, the real you, the only you on earth.

The years that spoil your gift wrap with other things more cruel,

should purify and strengthen and polish up that jewel.

So focus your attention on the inside, not the out, on being kinder,

wiser, more content, and more devout.

Then when your gift wrap is stripped away,

your jewel will be set free to radiate God's glory throughout eternity."

Acknowledgements:

I wish to thank my pastor, mentor, brother and friend, Bishop Larry A. Jackson, Regional Bishop, Fellowship of International Churches, Senior Pastor Bethel Outreach International Church, nationally know speaker and author of several books; *Beyond Reconciliation, Guilt Free Living, Knowing God by the Numbers, Numbered with the Transgressors, One Degree of Change, The Power is in the Closet, The True Value of a Woman, First Comes Love*; all available on Amazon. Without his continued support and spiritual guidance, this book would not be possible.

I also would like to give a heartfelt thank you to Mr. Rick Jennings, GIA Graduate Gemologist, Fellow, Gemological Association of Great Britain. Mr. Jennings graciously agreed to take the time to speak with me, share his knowledge and lend me some of his personal materials for further study.

www.ingramcontent.com/pod-product-compliance
Lightning Source LLC
Chambersburg PA
CBHW071644040426
42452CB00009B/1757